The Seed

Within

Discover and Cultivate Your
Purpose

Copyright: March, 2020

ISBN: 978-1-7348158-0-1

Insights Publishing

1550 Dogwood Dr. Rifle CO 81650

Edited by: Dr. Stephanie Stanfield

Forward by: Dr. Stephanie Stanfield

Dedication

To my Lord and Saviour Jesus Christ, thank you Lord for making me whole. Thank you, Lord, for my seed and for giving me the means to develop and cultivate it, that I might have an inspirational impact on others.

To my family for all their support through all my many endeavors. Especially my wife Sherri, who has seen my highs and lows and still stood behind me, and believed in me.

To Roaring Colorado Toastmasters for guiding me along my journey of public speaking. Without the group's guidance, I would not be the speaker I am today. Anyone who needs to speak in front of an audience should look into Toastmasters International.

To my direct sales company. Without you, I would not have even begun this journey. Your belief has become my belief, your dedication to the personal growth of every person in this company is an example of how all companies should be run. You are a beacon of light on the hill. Thank you, Angela and Phil.

Forward

The Seed

Within

Discover and Cultivate Your Purpose

I first met Bobby at a Roaring Colorado Toastmasters meeting. He was very personable and introduced himself to me because I was a guest.

Our small town had just finished a massive construction project of a bridge replacement just before I attended my first RCTM meeting. Our community was still reeling with the massive traffic impacts and disruptions to our lives.

I soon found out that Bobby had worked as a supervisor on that project. Knowing Bobby as I do now, he was growing his leadership and inspirational skills with that opportunity.

I watched as his increasing skill with interacting and engaging the audience kept pace with his soaring confidence. Once he steps on the podium, he owns the room. His presence is electric.

He competed in a TM district contest and won our area. No one in our club was surprised. We had all witnessed not only his personal growth but his professional growth that had occurred within a very short time. This is what's possible when you grow the seed within.

Bobby has honed his skill in motivating people with his speaking skills and keeping his audiences riveted. Now he is expressing his passion through inspirational writing.

I was honored to review Bobby's first book. I am doubly honored to be asked to write the forward. It isn't often that a person gets to be involved with someone so committed to a new passion. Now I am blessed to watch him work hard to successfully reap the benefits of his intensity and intention to become great.

I want to thank Bobby for allowing me to peek behind the curtain. I have been able to see all his hard work and dedication. That, in and of itself, is a great inspiration.

Dr. Stephanie Stanfield

Preface

I have spent a great many years wondering who I was and what my earthly purpose was. I have worked in several different career fields that range from law enforcement to civil construction. I have operated a couple of small businesses that were also very successful. However, it wasn't until I joined a network marketing company that I began to understand what my true direction was. I had always felt that my purpose has been to help other people. The network marketing company was also a service-oriented product. One thing about this company that quickly attracted me was, that beyond their desire to succeed financially, was their determination to help others simply to become better people. They know that by helping their distributors become better people, their sales will increase. This company expounds upon the theory of empowering its people to become better. Better parents, better friends, supervisors, co-workers, and yes, a better sales force.

They do this by promoting personal growth. Jim Rohn said, "Your level of success will seldom exceed your level of personal development because success is something you attract by the person you become." This company excels at this concept by promoting personal growth at every opportunity. This is one of the many reasons they have had multi-million dollar growth every year for the past 23 years.

This business model took me on a journey of self-discovery. I began to truly understand who I am. What my God-given earthly purpose is. I learned how to pursue that purpose and in the process discover the true joy in my life. I have gained knowledge and insight through years of studying personal growth. I am presenting you with a portion of that in this book.

My greatest wish for you is that you learn who you truly are and what your God-given purpose is, so that you may also find true joy.

Table of Contents

The Seed Within

Discover and Cultivate Your

Purpose

Bobby Branham

www.BobbyBranham.com

Chapter 1

How Many Seeds?

How many seeds do you think are in an apple? I have asked this question from the stage at several seminars and events. I get answers that have ranged from 3 or 4 to 15 or 20.

I asked my friend Google. Do you know Google? Google told me that on average there are 5 seeds in an apple. So, except for a few, most of the answers I have received were correct. Or at least close. I came to realize that the true question becomes not how many seeds are in an apple but how many apples will come from one of those seeds. As I thought about seeds from this different perspective, it appears that you will need to plant the seed in some good soil, give it some water, some fertilizers, lots of sunshine, and pull the weeds. Then, allow the tree to grow and mature, which can take between six and ten years. Once the tree matures, that single seed will ultimately produce hundreds of thousands of apples.

That got me to thinking about another seed, the seed within us. You see we all have a God-given purpose in life. That's our seed within. God planted that seed within us, we are the good soil. It's our job to cultivate that seed. We have to provide the water, the fertilizer, and the sunshine that our seed needs to grow.

God told us about this in Jesus' parable of the sower. He said that some of the seeds fell by the wayside and the birds gobbled them up. Those are the people who pay no attention to the potential they have within them.

He said some fell on rocky ground and were scorched by the sun. Those are people with a hardness of heart.

He said that some fell among the thorns. Those are the people who are easily influenced and follow every whim.

He said that others fell upon good ground and brought forth fruit in abundance. These are the people who are cultivating their seed. These are the people who are working to better themselves, thereby creating good soil. They are the ones producing the fruits that God intended for them. They have found true joy.

You are not here just to exist. You are not here just to get a job, pay bills, die, and fade away. You have a purpose. You have a reason for being. How do you tap into that? How do you cultivate that seed? How do you make yourself the fertile soil so that you will produce an abundance of fruit? In the Bible, the book of Joshua 1:8 says *"This book of the law shall not depart out of thy mouth; but thou shalt meditate therein day and night, that thou mayest observe to do according to all that is written therein: for then thou shalt make thy way prosperous, and then thou shalt have good success."*

In this quote, Joshua is talking about the Pentateuch, the first 5 books of the Bible written by Moses. To paraphrase, learn the book of the law, study it, and live by it. Then you shall be successful.

Earl Nightingale once said, "If you will study, one extra hour, every day, in your chosen field, that within 5 years or less. You will become a national expert in that field." Think about that, a national expert. What could you do or become if you only studied half an hour a day?

I know you may be thinking "Hey look, you don't know my life. You don't know how busy I am. I work long hours! I'm up at 5 and on the road by 6. I'm at work by 7. I work 10 hours and I work hard! Then I'm not home until 6! Then it's the demands of the kid's homework, dinner, dishes, baths, and the next thing I know it's 9! And, I have to go to bed because the next day I have to do it all over again!"

Is this your story? If this is what you tell yourself. Then I'm here to tell you, that's a load of crap. You are lying to yourself. You are making up excuses for the mediocrity in your life. You are your own enabler.

Everybody has 24 hours in a day. Everybody has 168 hours in a week. What you do with that time is up to you! How much time do you spend on social media? How much time do you spend playing video games? How much time do you spend watching TV? What you do with your time is up to you!

You may ask, then how do I do it. How do I fit bettering myself into the time I don't have?

That's the beauty of technology. If you have a commute that is more than 5-10 minutes, you can start there! Begin by making your commute your learning time. Download audiobooks and podcasts. Listen and learn.

If you like to read, read more. If you don't like to read, start reading anyway. Reading is great! But, don't just read for the sake of reading. Study, learn, and devour your books.

Almost all of my books have words, sentences, and paragraphs underlined or highlighted. I write comments in the margins. Why? Because when you interact with the information you are reading, the process becomes more effective. You will retain and comprehend more than if you just read. This is why we are made to write book reports in school. It reinforces what we have read.

You may ask, "What if I don't know what my seed is? What if I don't know what to learn?

I highly recommend that you start learning about anything that gives a positive light. Start with your Bible. A friend once told me that the word bible was an acronym. He said it meant Basic Instructions Before Leaving Earth. Learn about communication, teamwork, and leadership.

Does mountain climbing; cooking, skiing, woodworking, or sandcastle building, interest you? Any of these topics can be found in books.

Go into any bookstore or website that sells books and you will find multiple volumes of books on any subject you choose. Listen to or read biographies on great influential people like JFK, Thomas Jefferson, or Winston Churchill.

Get out and do things. Go places you have never visited or explored before. Experience things you have never done before.

As you do these activities then your seed, your purpose, will reveal itself to you. That is when you will start to realize where you will find true joy. Not happiness but joy. Happiness comes and goes, joy is everlasting.

I believe you want to feel joy. Everybody wants to feel true joy. Even the panhandler on the street corner wants to be successful and feel joy in his heart. It's true! Think about it! If the panhandler makes $20.00 today, don't you think that tomorrow he will be back out there? Doing his best to look more needy, more down and out. Don't you think he may try a different sign that will deliver a different message? Because maybe, just maybe, this time he can make $30 or even $40.00? It's not an easy road. Everybody has to work for it. The question is. Are you willing to do what it takes to achieve what you want? Everybody stumbles, everybody falls, everybody fails. The question is will you get back up? Will you learn, will you grow? Being successful and finding joy is not a destination it's a journey. It's who you become along the way. Do you want to produce an abundance of apples? Think like the tree! Think like the person you would like to be. Ask yourself, how would the person I would like to be, do the thing that I want to do? Then nurture your seed! Make the decision! Nothing happens until a decision is made. Finding and following your purpose will bring joy into your life. Joy is the essence of success.

Chapter 2

The Seed

Jesus talked about the parable of the sower. He told how some seeds fell by the wayside and the birds got them. He told how some fell on rocky ground and the sun scorched them. Then he told how some fell among the thorns and were choked. Finally, he told how some seeds fell on good ground and they grew and produced fruit.

What is a seed? A seed represents the very first spark that has the potential to light a wildfire. It is the beginning, the nucleus which contains all the information necessary to become everything possible.

When we think of seeds any number of things may come to mind. A seed all by itself will normally not accomplish very much. As the parable of the sower, suggests. The seed needs something else, something more. Yet the seed contains within it, everything that it has the potential to become. Everything about the seed is dependent on what is added to it. What happens to our lawns during drought years when we are put under water rationing? It turns brown. What happens to our lawn when we can give plenty of water and fertilizer? It grows a lush green.

Seeds are the lifeblood of our world. Not only do they bring forth food. They are also the nucleus of ideas and concepts. When man first looked to the stars in wonder, a seed was planted. Around 2000 BC. One man looked upon the stars and marveled at them. So much so, that he would stay up late every night so that he could study their movements. Night after night this went on. This man was a very important man among his people. When he told others about his fascination with the stars, many of them also began to gaze upon them. Others thought nothing of it and went about their days. Some were hunters, others teachers, and still others makers of pottery. Night after night, this important man and the others who felt as he did would study those stars. While following their movements through the night sky, they began to see a correlation between the passage of time and the movement of the stars.

They created a methodology of chronicling the passage of time. This methodology of measuring time created thousands of years ago is more accurate than our current calendar system.

The Mayan calendar chronicled time until December 21, 2012. This is the date that their long count calendar of 5125 years ended and a new long count calendar would begin to be used.

Similarly, around 600 BC., on the other side of the world, another man was pondering the stars. He too marveled at their movement in the night sky. As he gazed upon them, he noticed that their movement seemed to be concentric. Almost as if they were circling the earth itself. This, along with the study of the phases and shape of the moon, gave

Pythagoras the idea that the earth was a sphere and not flat.

Around 400 BC., the seed of astronomy and the concept of a spherical earth continued to grow in the mind of Plato. In 300 BC., the same seed grew in the mind of Aristotle.

That seed germinated in many people. Generation after generation it has grown. Men began to notice how they could predict that movement. This led to the navigation of ships upon the ocean. It became possible for man to sail upon the ocean for months at a time without ever seeing land, plotting his course utilizing the stars, and their predictable movement.

Today we know that the earth is round. We understand how the solar system works, with its planets revolving around the sun. Through our increased knowledge of mathematics and the application of science, we can formulate how our galaxy functions.

In my lifetime man has walked on the moon, created an International Space Station, sent rovers to Mars, and created the fifth military branch, This fifth branch is known as the United States Space Force. All this happened because a seed of curiosity, about the stars, began to grow in the hearts and minds of men.

There is an average, of 5 seeds in any given apple. Each one of those seeds has the potential to produce a tree that will, in turn, produce hundreds of thousands of apples. Just as the seed of curiosity about the stars, grew in the hearts and minds of thousands of people over thousands of years. One such seed may produce a tree that does not receive the full amount of nutrients that it needs while another seed from the same apple may be planted in rich fertile soil and given all of the sunshine and water that it needs. That tree goes on to produce an abundance of fruit for years and years to come, while the first tree only produces a fraction of that. Both seeds had the same initial potential the only difference is what was added to them.

This reminds me of the 1988 movie "Twins" starring Arnold Schwarzenegger and Danny DeVito. The two men are unknowingly part of a science experiment. They are separated at birth. One is raised with all of the best things in life while the other is not.

Schwarzenegger's character (Julius) grows up on a peaceful island where the weather is always beautiful. He is provided with the finest education and grows up in a kind and loving environment.

DeVito's character (Vincent) grows up in an inner-city orphanage environment. He has a hard life, having to fight for everything he has. For the sake of the movie, two very opposite men are cast for the parts. But the true contrast is to see how each one grew and what kind of person each one became, because of the environment.

One was cast among the thorns and the other fell on good ground. However just because one seed, or in the case of Schwarzenegger and DeVito, one gets off to a poor start, does not mean that the poorly underdeveloped one, cannot recover and become just as fruitful and the first.

Chapter 3

The Seed Within

Our seed within is given by God. In the book of John 3:27, it says, *"A man can receive nothing, except it be given him from heaven."* Each one of us is uniquely different. There is no one size fits all. Even identical twins have differences that allow us to tell them apart.

We all have a God-given purpose and that purpose is uniquely different to all of us. Sure, some may be similar but ultimately they are all different.

Every person wants to find himself, to know who he is, somewhere, and somehow to know his identity. When you discover your purpose, then you have found your true self. And in finding yourself you discover that which brings you true joy.

In 1993 the movie Tombstone was released. In 1994 the movie Wyatt Earp was released. Both movies told a similar story yet each was different.

Identical twins share similarities yet each is different. Millions of people can play the same musical instrument. Yet each person will have their own unique individual style even when playing the same song. There is nothing wrong with this. In fact, it is a wonderful thing.

Currently, there are an estimated 100 billion galaxies in the universe. None of these is exactly like. Within any given galaxy there are an estimated 100 thousand million stars and an estimated 100 billion planets.

On our planet, there are approximately 7.4 billion people. Not a single person is identical to another. Fingerprint and iris recognition technology are effective means of security on our phone and other applications because no two are exactly alike.

In the 1991 movie Robin Hood starring Kevin Costner and Morgan Freeman, there is a scene in which a little girl asks Morgan Freeman's character. "Did God paint you?" To which he replies, "yes." The little girl then asks "why?" His reply sums it all up. "Because Ala (God) loves wondrous variety."

The seed that is within you is unique to you. You are the good soil and God loves wondrous variety. While the seed within you may be similar to that of another, it will still be uniquely different. That is what makes each one of us special.

Because you are uniquely different from any other person on the planet, the seed within will produce different fruit.

As I mentioned in chapter one, two seeds from the same apple can produce a lesser or greater fruit.

I have two brothers; we were all predominantly raised by our mother. Yes, the poor woman had to raise three boys by herself. Being the oldest my role should have been to help her. I should have aspired to be the man of the house.

Instead, I was a bit of a trouble maker all through school. I drank, smoked marijuana, skipped school. I was part of the rough crowd, leather jacket, t-shirt, 501 button fly jeans with a cut in the seam at the cuff. I managed to graduate anyway.

Then I enlisted in the Marine Corps and this decision ultimately turned my life around. My middle brother followed in my footsteps, spending time with the same type of delinquent crowd. Except for enlisting in the military, he ultimately turned his life around as well.

My youngest brother graduated from high school and went on to college, received his degree, and became a Physical Therapist.

Now he is a business owner and operates a physical training facility.

We all received the same upbringing yet each one of us turned out differently. And yet, we have all become successful in life.

Chapter 4

Fertilizer

Fertilizer is defined as a material that is applied to the soil or plant tissues, to supply nutrients needed for growth. Just as we fertilize our organic plants we also need to fertilize our minds.

My middle brother and I are similar in many ways. We pursue many of the same interests and yet our outcomes are different.

My youngest brother has gone down a completely different path and his outcomes are different. What causes these differences? The base soil is the same yet we are all unique.

I am two years older than my middle brother and six years older than my youngest. The external influences we experienced growing up were different for each of us. Even though, we all went to the same elementary school, the same middle school, and the same high school. Each of us had different friends, different teachers, and different social and economic circumstances in our lives. Those external influences became the nutrients our seeds received.

To better illustrate this I'll tell you about Jacob. Jacob is a young man 23 years old. He is tall at 6'2" with dark hair neatly kept and a slender build. The process of analytics has always fascinated him. He is the youngest to graduate from Harvard University with a Ph.D. in analytics.

In addition to his fascination with analytics, Jacob has always loved to tinker and invent items for himself and others. After graduation, he inquires about a job listed in the local paper. The ad read "Seeking individual with excellent analytical skills for self-starter, self-motivated position. Pay commensurate with experience." Jacob immediately applies for the position and upon review of his credentials is hired on the spot.

His new employer tells him that the position will be running an information repository. His job description is to collect the incoming data, file it, and interpret any meaningful patterns and relationships in the data.

On his first day, he enters his main office. The room is spacious, square, and about 20' by 20'. The walls are white with no windows to see outside. Along one wall is a door. In front of the door, is an old-style wooden desk, and a very comfortable looking black leather office chair. The desk is beautifully polished with no smears or scratches. There is no phone or lamp. Only a large computer monitor, mouse, and keyboard.

Jacob takes a seat in the chair and finds it to be the most comfortable chair he has ever sat in. As he looks to the wall facing him, he notices three state of the art printers. As he looks to the left and right, each wall has one printer. Above each of the five printers is an empty document frame.

He rises from his luxurious chair to further inspect the printers. Each printer is silver in color with state of the art touch panels. Each printer has its own LAN cable plugged into the wall. Oddly there is no scanner, fax, or e-mail function built into the printers. Each printer has a single flashing green light with a label beside it that says "standby". All is quiet.

Jacob decides to inspect what is beyond the door behind his desk. He surmises it must be the repository. He reaches for the door handle, turns it, and easily pushes the door open. The room is dark, nothing can be seen within. As he steps inside the room large lights on the ceiling begin to flicker on. First, he sees a set of six directly above him. Then he sees another set of six, 20 feet further down on the ceiling. Then another set of six another 20 feet further down into the room. Then another and another until fifteen sets of six lights, 20 feet apart, have become illuminated.

The room is the size of a football field. As the lights become brighter he sees that the room is filled with row after row of filing cabinets, double stacked. Each filing cabinet appears empty and is without a label. Jacob opens one of the filing cabinet drawers and finds it to be filled with blank hanging folders and blank file folders. He inspects another and another finding them all to be the same.

Now Jacob isn't sure exactly what this job is going to entail. Jacob heads back to the office room with all the printers. As he enters the room there is an eerie silence that fills the room. He takes a seat in the luxurious chair. As he starts to relax and almost drift off to sleep. He hears a soft tone come from one of the printers. Beep, beep. Suddenly the printer on the left wall lights up and a single sheet of paper emerges.

Excited that his job is beginning, Jacob leaps out of the chair rushes over to the printer.

He is confused as he reads only two words on the document. "Gurgle, gurgle." In addition to the words, he also sees a timestamp with the current date and time. Not fully understanding what is going on he returns to his desk.

Just as he sits down again and places the paper on the desk the printer on the right wall lights up and begins printing. Again Jacob leaps to his feet to see what the document says. "Warm" is the only word printed on the paper.

Weeks go by; the only printers that are active are the ones to the left and right. Always the same type of information. "Warm"; "Soft", "Comfortable", from the other, "Ba-boom, Ba-boom, Ba-boom", "Gurgle-Gurgle", "Pshhh-pop-pop". None of it makes any sense.

Jacob is almost at his wits end not understanding what to do. Where is the analytics in any of this? He is about to quit this job. It's nothing like he was told it would be.

Then one day a different message from the printer on the right, **"SQUEEZED!!!"**. Then a few minutes later again, **"SQUEEZED!!!"**. For hours this goes on, always the same, big bold letters **"SQUEEZED!!!"**. Jacob places the papers with the others on the desk, trying to make some sort of sense out of it all. "How do they all fit together?" He asks himself.

Suddenly all of the printers in the room light up and begin printing. The three printers on the far wall that have never printed anything are spitting out page after page!

The printers to the left and right are doing the same! So many pages are coming from the printers that they begin to pile up on the floor! Page after page after page, full of words every page! The space in front of the desk is beginning to fill with papers! Where are they all coming from he wonders? Just as suddenly as all of the chaos began, it all stops.

The room is once again quiet. As Jacob inspects the printers again only the green lights are flashing next to the word "standby".

As Jacob examines the piles of papers on the floor he sees that he has his work cut out for him. He begins first by organizing the papers into stacks on his desk in relation to the printer that they came from.

Then he sorts them in accordance with the time stamp. Since he has already accumulated some information from the left and right printers he begins with them. All of the documents that came from the printer are the left read. "Ahhhh!" "You're doing great!"

"Just one more!" All the documents from the printer on the right read. "Squeezed!" "Cold," "pressure," "dry." "Warm," soft," "comfortable." From the front wall the center printer; "Bright", "blurry." From the printer to the left of the center. "Blech!" "Mmmmm," "Savory". Lastly the printer to the right of the center, "Aroma!", "Essence", "Clean", "Pheromone."

Jacob looks at the five stacks of papers. He knows there has to be a relationship between them all. What could it be, he wonders.

From the right-hand desk drawer, he pulls out five blank pieces of paper. He places each one on the desk above the individual stack from the printers. There is something about them. What is it? Looking at the stacks of papers from left to right. He picks up the stack on the right and as he reads each page he realizes something. Every word describes a sound! Jacob takes the blank page from above the stack and with a large black magic marker he writes. "HEARING".

He picks up the next stack which represents the left printer from the front wall. Looking through the pages, all the words describe elements of the palate. He takes the blank page and writes "TASTE".

Checking the third stack from the center printer he writes "SIGHT". On the next stack of papers, he writes "SMELL".

For the last stack, from the printer on the right wall, he labels it as "TOUCH". The printers are sending information from the five senses! As Jacob places each of the papers in the document frames above their respective printers he begins to understand his new position. He realizes this will be a life-long project.

He starts to work by inputting the data into the computer. Then, he begins setting up the filing cabinets in the repository. Just as he is finishing, and sits down for a well-deserved rest.

Suddenly, all of the printers come to life again! This time they run for a little longer and each page contains more and more information. Then just as suddenly as everything began, it all stops and all is quiet.

Once again Jacob begins to correlate and input the data from all the papers. This process repeats itself again and again. Jacob decides it would be helpful to automate some of the processes he is doing.

He creates five small bots. One bot represents each printer. The bots are programmed to read the page. If the information is similar to previous information, the bot files the page in the repository along with the previous similar information.

If the information is new, the bot will deliver the page to Jacob's desk so that Jacob can enter the data and develop the relationship between the other senses.

This story of Jacob is a light comparison of how the subconscious mind works. When we are born our minds are a blank slate. While we are awake, everything that we are exposed to is entered is received. As we sleep, everything is classified and filed away. As we are exposed to more and more experiences, our subconscious mind begins to link different elements of those experiences together.

We may hear the word "hot". We are not able to associate anything with that word or concept until we touch something "hot". Now our mind links together physical pain with touching something "hot".

In the same type of example, we can also associate hot with the sun as being comfortable while beaming down on us as we lie on the beach. This, in turn, engages the survival mechanism of staying away from pain by not touching something "hot" or moving toward the pleasure of lying on the beach on a "hot" summer day.

In this same way, we begin to create core values by living our experiences. These values are deeply rooted in our psyche and determine who we are as a person. However, just because these values come into existence from birth does not mean that they cannot be changed. Or that new ones cannot be created.

On any given day we make approximately 35,000 decisions. All of these decisions are based on our learned values and emotions. Most of these decisions are made on autopilot. These unconscious choices are similar to the popular program IFTT, (If This Then That). Or it works like the bots that Jacob created.

To change the decisions we make, we have to change or adjust our values. We have to reprogram the bots. These values are a major element of your seed. In chapter one, I said that if you will just begin to read anything positive and encouraging your seed will reveal itself to you.

This is because the subconscious mind will assimilate what you have read and attach it to a value. The more you read of the same type of material, the stronger that value will become. You will begin to see certain topics have more appeal. You will find yourself seeking more and more on your new-found favorite topics. Your seed is revealing itself to you, and you are receiving joy from it.

Chapter 5

Pull the weeds

Earlier I mentioned that you must feed your seed with good nutrients and pull the weeds. The weeds will steal the good away from the seed.

What are the weeds? The weeds are negativity. Anything that is composed of negativity is a weed.

How do you pull it? You replace it with something positive. While we are young we don't have very much ability to control the influences to which we are exposed. Those influences will have a positive or negative impact on us.

Recently, I watched a video going viral on the internet. It showed a little Irish girl sitting at a table. She said, "my head." The person running the camera asked, "Who hit your head?" The girl says "Chucky, f----ng Chucky!"

Because this video quickly went viral, it's obvious that a lot of people thought it was really funny. I even found a response where one person said they were going to start a cult following of this little girl.

This is a prime example of how we are influenced by events and circumstances in our lives. This little girl obviously has an influential person in her life that regularly uses profanity.

Unfortunately, it is most likely an influence that she cannot avoid. While she may be developing a following now, it may not be the type of following she will be excited about later in life.

The good news is that we can change those influences and pull out those weeds. As we keep weeding and we begin to nurture our seed with positivity rather than negativity, then things will begin to change.

Every one of us can direct our life path. Once you start, you may find that you begin to crave the new information. Only you can decide to pull the weeds. Only you can replace the negativity with good positive fertilizer.

Reading is one of the easiest ways to fertilize your seed. It is also the least expensive and most beneficial.

Reading helps the mind to grow. Reading takes you to places in your mind's eye that you may never get to physically visit. Reading solves problems that you have not yet faced. Reading motivational and advice filled books makes you a better supervisor, a better business owner, a better employee, even a better spouse. Whether you read, Zig Ziglar's "Secrets of Closing the Sale", or Janet Evanovich's Stephanie Plum series, these books will benefit you in almost all areas of your life.

You may be asking yourself, how can a fiction novel about a female private detective, help me be a better supervisor at work? Because at some point in life, at work, at home, or church, you may encounter a similar situation that can be resolved in the same way a fictional character handled it.

You may not even consciously remember the passage you read. But your sub-conscience remembers and then can apply that knowledge to the current situation.

When you read, whether fiction or non-fiction you absorb knowledge from the writer. Thus, we become a student of the author. How would it feel to be able to say that you are a student of Jesus Christ, Plato, George Washington, Thomas Jefferson, Abraham Lincoln, Winston Churchill, Dale Carnegie, JFK? In my opinion, these are just a few of the greatest minds. Through reading their original writings or studies of them, we can learn from them.

My wife loves to watch true-crime TV. Shows like "Forensic Files" and "Cold Case Files". We tease each other that she is learning how to commit the perfect murder. The truth of the matter is that a lot of knowledge can be gained from watching these types of shows.

Don't misunderstand; I'm not condoning watching television in place of reading. But what if, God forbid, you walked into a crime scene. Having watched some true crime shows in the past you now have a solid knowledge that the worst thing you could do is contaminate the scene.

I remember watching one episode of "Forensic Files" with my wife, where a woman was trying desperately to get her innocent husband out of prison. He had been tried and found guilty for murder.

The woman had been watching the show and gained knowledge of how to collect and handle DNA evidence. She began to conduct her own investigation into the murder. She properly collected DNA evidence, had it tested at an authorized lab, and upon receiving the results, she presented the evidence to the court.

As a result of all of her efforts, her husband was released!

This was a very unique situation and I do not recommend that anyone go out and conduct a criminal investigation. It does, however, show that knowledge is valuable and knowledge is powerful. Without applying and using the knowledge she gained by watching the show, her husband would still be serving a prison sentence for a crime he did not commit.

This goes to show that true wealth comes from knowledge. Knowledge creates value. Would you like to get a raise at work? Become more valuable to your employer. Take it upon yourself to learn more about the position you hold. Ask questions. Attend a seminar or webinar.

Many employers will even pay for you to attend a training event because they know that if you perform your job better, they will reap the benefits too. This is one of the methods used by top performers to become top performers. Whether your employer pays for additional training or not it is worth the investment. If your current employer doesn't appreciate the improvements in yourself that you have made, another one will. They will most likely be willing to pay more for your abilities.

I spent many years in the field of civil construction. I wanted to learn how to operate heavy equipment. Every opportunity that came available I used to learn more about, and become more proficient in operating different types of equipment. When a supervisor asked me to complete a certain task, I would also ask to see the blueprint drawings so that I could fully understand the task at hand. In doing this I learned how to proficiently read blueprints.

Once I understood how to read blueprints, and became proficient on several pieces of heavy equipment. I was allowed to run small projects on my own without supervision. I began working two or three laborers under my supervision. I began completing tasks both proficiently and efficiently.

This, in turn, led to a promotion from Lead Operator to Foreman. My promotion included a substantial pay raise. I made myself more valuable to my employer and was properly compensated for it. My employer didn't want my expertise to go to another company.

After working for a couple of years as a Foreman, with a crew of three to four operators and a half dozen laborers, I was elevated to a Superintendent position. I was required to run an entire project from start to finish, supervising three Foremen and all of their crews. This wasn't something that happened overnight. It took several years to accomplish.

I later went on to run a County Road and Bridge District, managing a crew of 13 operators, maintaining 250 lane miles of road, conducting county-wide bridge inspections. Part of this job requirement was to be a construction inspector for projects conducted in my district by the construction company that previously employed me. During this time I continued attending more education and training seminars to keep expanding my knowledge base.

I could have allowed the weeds of negativity to grow and choke out my potential. I could have spent more time jumping on the complaining bandwagon. I could have spent too much time agreeing with others about how this or that was not fair.

Instead, I dealt with negative experiences and made the best of them. I kept the weeds of negativity out and keep feeding the nutrients of good useful knowledge. Ultimately, I started my trucking business, and later a profitable Network Marketing business.

Chapter 6

Joy Equals Success

The interesting thing about a seed is that it wants to grow. My wife once left a small clove of garlic on the counter for several days. Without any water or fertilizer, it began to sprout. When you leave potatoes in a dark pantry for several days, roots will begin to grow. It's the survival mechanism that is built into every living thing. It's the drive to succeed.

Every living thing wants to succeed. That clove of garlic will begin to grow on the kitchen counter because of its internal mechanism that says "grow, produce, be successful". In the same way, our internal mechanism to survive says to be successful at it. After all, the result of not being successful at survival is, not surviving.

In chapter one, I used the example of a panhandler to show that it doesn't make a difference who you are or what your situation is in life. There is an internal drive to be successful at whatever you are doing. That internal mechanism says "come out on top", "achieve more", "be better". The truly interesting thing about success is that only you can define what success is for you.

I worked with a man at a construction company. We were both foremen for the company. Each of us took pride in the work that we accomplished. I enjoyed my job. I felt the satisfaction of completing a project from start to finish. It felt good to see what was once a vacant lot, transformed into a shopping center or a new home.

However, I wanted to do and be more. I had dreams of owning my own company.

Having my equipment my employees and my contracts.

I once asked my friend; "Aren't you tired of working for someone else? Aren't you tired of making him a ton of money?" My friend said he loved his job, that it gave him satisfaction. He said he didn't care if the owner of the company had a private plane and was living in a big fancy house.

My friend lived in a small cabin in a very small neighboring town. He had a Harley Davidson motorcycle and a small pickup truck. He was able to drive a company truck to and from work. He felt great about the projects he had completed. He said that years after a project was completed he could drive by and feel a sense of accomplishment. He didn't want the headaches and hassles of employees, insurance, equipment breakdowns, and bidding on projects.

He was happy, he was fulfilled and he was successful. His definition of success was different than mine. I know that your definition will also be different than mine or his.

He found his joy. He wasn't even concerned about how much money he was making. He enjoyed what he was doing so much that the amount of money he was taking home didn't matter. He was making enough to take care of his needs and that was sufficient.

When I first started with my local Toastmasters group I always felt great after each meeting. Each meeting was such fun that I didn't want it to end. As I would walk to my car I felt on top of the world. I was discovering my purpose.

One of the most satisfying things for me is to hear from someone in my audience about how what I had to say touched them. It felt great to hear that what I said has had an impact on them. During one of the first speaking competitions with my local Toastmasters group, I won first place. I then went on to compete at a regional group. Again, I won first place. This win meant that I would next compete at the state level.

In that competition, I was sure that I was going to beat out the other speakers. My wife and I believed that my speech was far better than the others. Upon the announcement of the winners, I didn't even place. I was dismayed and upset that I didn't win. As my wife and I were leaving the event, I was approached by a man who had attended the event.

He stopped me and thanked me for my speech. He told me how he got so much meaning from it and how he didn't understand why I didn't take first place. At that moment I felt a tingling chill run through my body, suddenly winning or losing that competition didn't matter. Winning that competition was no longer what was important. I thanked him for his comments. As my wife and I walked to the car. I told her how winning the competition no longer mattered. What mattered was that I had made a difference in that man's life.

Another time I was speaking on a team call with my direct sales company. A few weeks later I was at a group event and was approached by a team member who had been on that call. She told me how much she enjoyed that call, how what I said, had such an impact on her. Once again there was that full-body tingling chill running through me.

I was not monetarily compensated for either of those talks. I was compensated with the joy of knowing that I had made a difference in those people's lives. When you have found your purpose, money is no longer the objective. The objective becomes fulfilling that purpose, you then become the objective of the money.

I once had the privilege of seeing DeVon Franklin speak at a convention. DeVon told his story of how he pursued a career in Hollywood. His dream was to make a change in Hollywood for the better. He started out working as an assistant to Will Smith. As time went on he later created Franklin Entertainment, becoming a producer himself and having Will Smith work for him.

Franklin's dream is to make a difference by creating good wholesome movies. His main mission is to make movies that do not rely on sex, drugs, foul language, and violence to make a profit. He produces movies that gave a clear positive message and have a positive impact on others. His pursuit was never about how much money he could make. His pursuit was about how much of a difference he could make.

He has now become an incredibly successful, producer, author, and speaker. DeVon Franklin is fulfilling his purpose and experiencing true joy in the process.

The definition of success is different for everyone. Only you can decide what that definition is. When you find your purpose, your reason for being, you will wake up without an alarm. You'll find that you can't wait to get started every day.

One thing is for certain, you will know when you have found success because you will also have found true joy. As you look back on how you became successful you will see that the success you now feel is a direct result of the person you have become.

That is the kind of success that no one can take away from you. It has been given to you by God. It is the fruit brought forth by developing and cultivating The Seed Within.

Bobby has been involved in public speaking since 2015. He has been a student of personal growth since 2013 and he continues to study to this day. Bobby says, "You can never stop learning about yourself and the people around you." His enthusiasm and love for people are what make him an excellent speaker. He has found joy in life, and that joy comes from inspiring others.

Inquire about Bobby's speaking availability or his direct sales business at:

www.BobbyBranham.com

www.ingramcontent.com/pod-product-compliance
Lightning Source LLC
Chambersburg PA
CBHW020553030426
42337CB00013B/1081